Favorite Classical Themes for Ukulele

by David Coe

© 2018 by Mel Bay Publications, Inc. All Rights Reserved.

WWW.MELBAY.COM

Preface

I hope you enjoy this collection of popular classical pieces arranged for ukulele in high or low G tuning (GCEA). The melodies are written in both standard notation and tablature with chord diagrams included. All of the melodies are arranged to be played on the first three strings, with the fourth string used only in chords.

This book will serve as an introduction to the classics for beginners and is a great source for more advanced players who would like to add songs by the great composers to their melody/chord repertoire.

Thanks to Jim Clark for his technical assistance in the preparation of this book.

David Coe

About the Author

David Coe

David Coe is the author of two guitar books for Mel Bay Publications, Inc. *Building Guitar Speed* and *Guitarists Treasury of Classic Themes.*

He has been teaching and performing on guitar and ukulele for over 25 years, sharing the stage with many well-known artists. He is a member of the music faculty at Fairfield University and The Unquowa School, both in Fairfield CT.

Contents

Minuet

Arranged by David Coe

J. S. Bach
Christian Petzold

Gavotte

Arranged by David Coe

J. S. Bach

Für Elise

Arranged by David Coe

Ludwig van Beethoven

Am
E7
N.C.
Am
E7
N.C.
Am
E7
Am
Am
E7
Am
N.C.
Am
E7
Am
N.C.
Am
E7
Am

Ode to Joy

Arranged by David Coe

Ludwig van Beethoven

Lullaby

Arranged by David Coe

Johannes Brahms

Turkish March

Arranged by David Coe

Ludwig van Beethoven

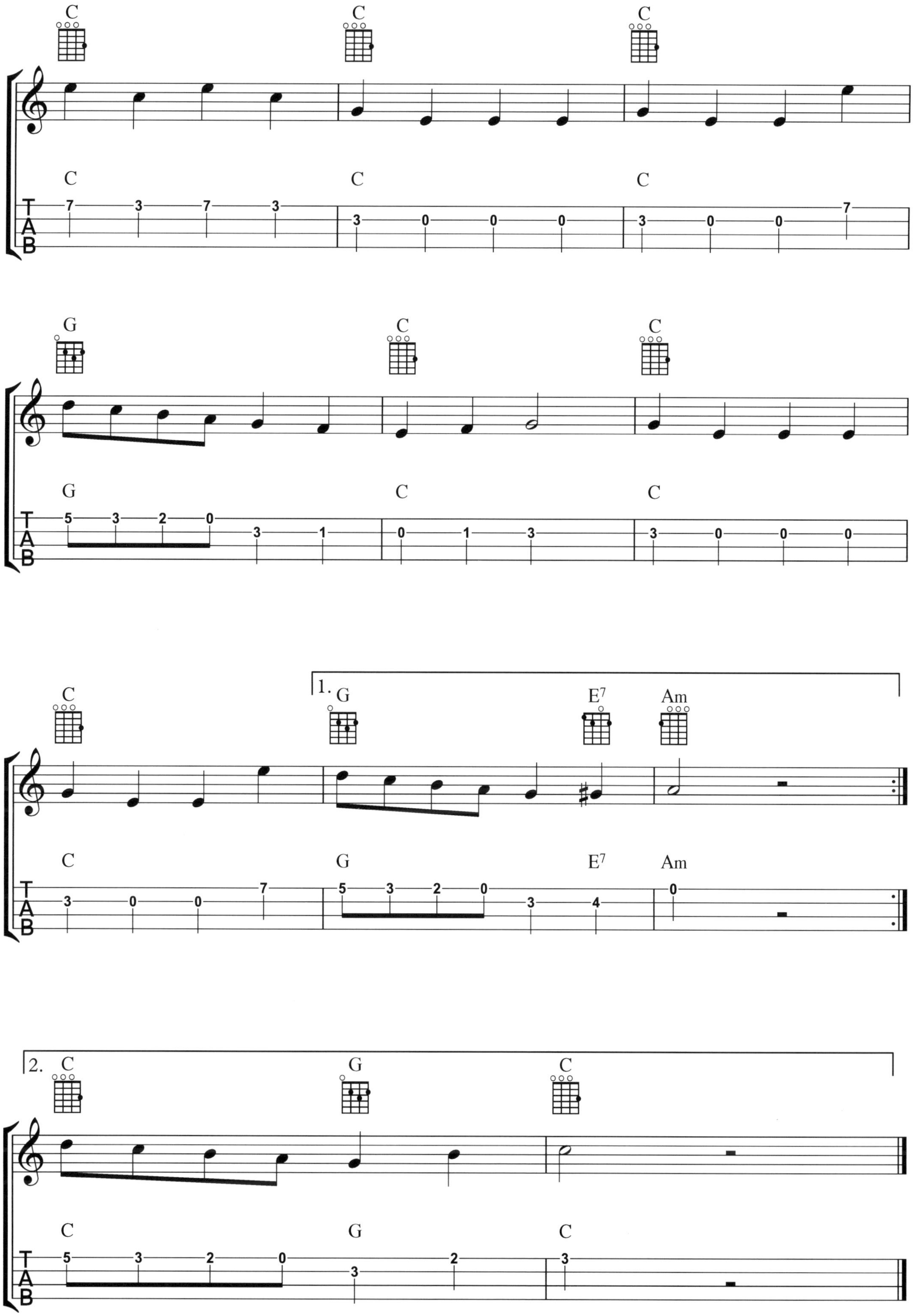
C C C
C C C
G C C
G C C
C 1. G E7 Am
C G E7 Am
2. C G C
C G C

Waltz

Arranged by David Coe

Ferdinando Carulli

C F C7
F F B♭
C7 F F
B♭ C7 F
TAB

Largo

Arranged by David Coe

Antonín Dvořák

In the Hall of the Mountain King

Arranged by David Coe

Edvard Grieg

Surprise Symphony

Arranged by David Coe

Franz Joseph Haydn

Rondeau

Arranged by David Coe

Jean - Joseph Mouret

The Entertainer

Arranged by David Coe

Scott Joplin

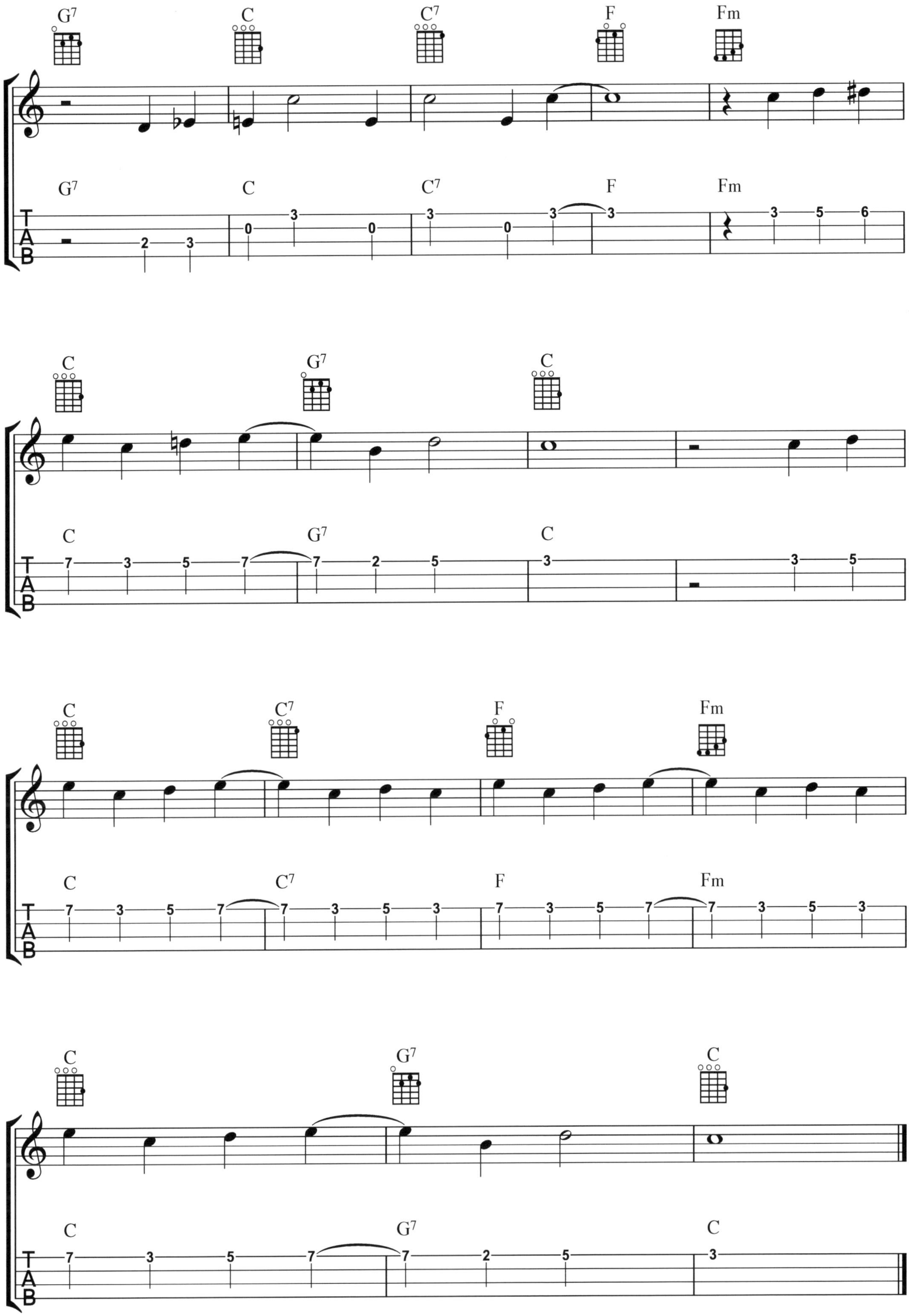
G7 C C7 F Fm
C G7 C
C C7 F Fm
C G7 C
TAB

The Merry Widow Waltz

Arranged by David Coe

Franz Lehár

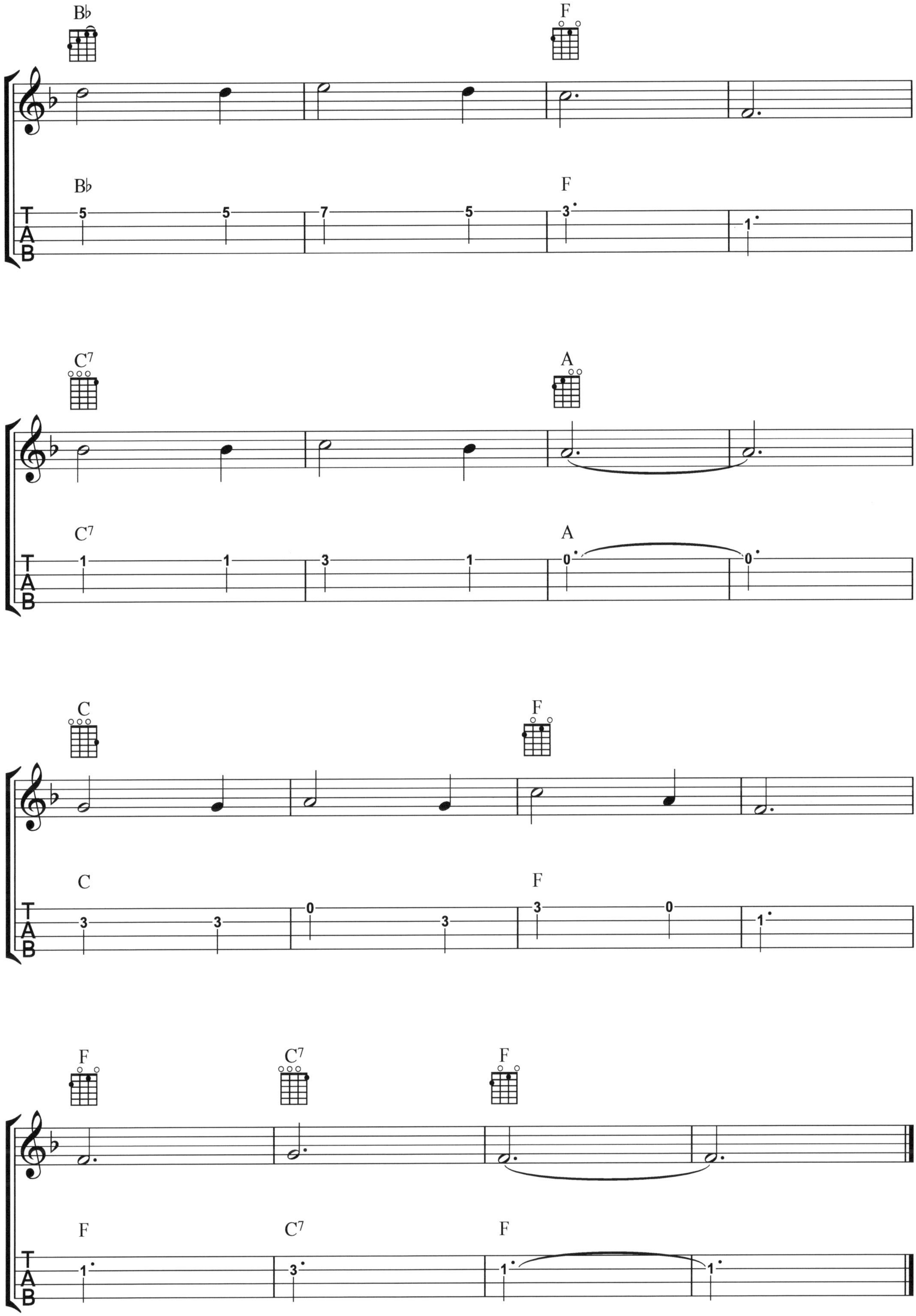
B♭ F
B♭ F
C7 A
C7 A
C F
C F
F C7 F
F C7 F

Eine Kleine Nachtmusik

Arranged by David Coe

Wolfgang Amadeus Mozart

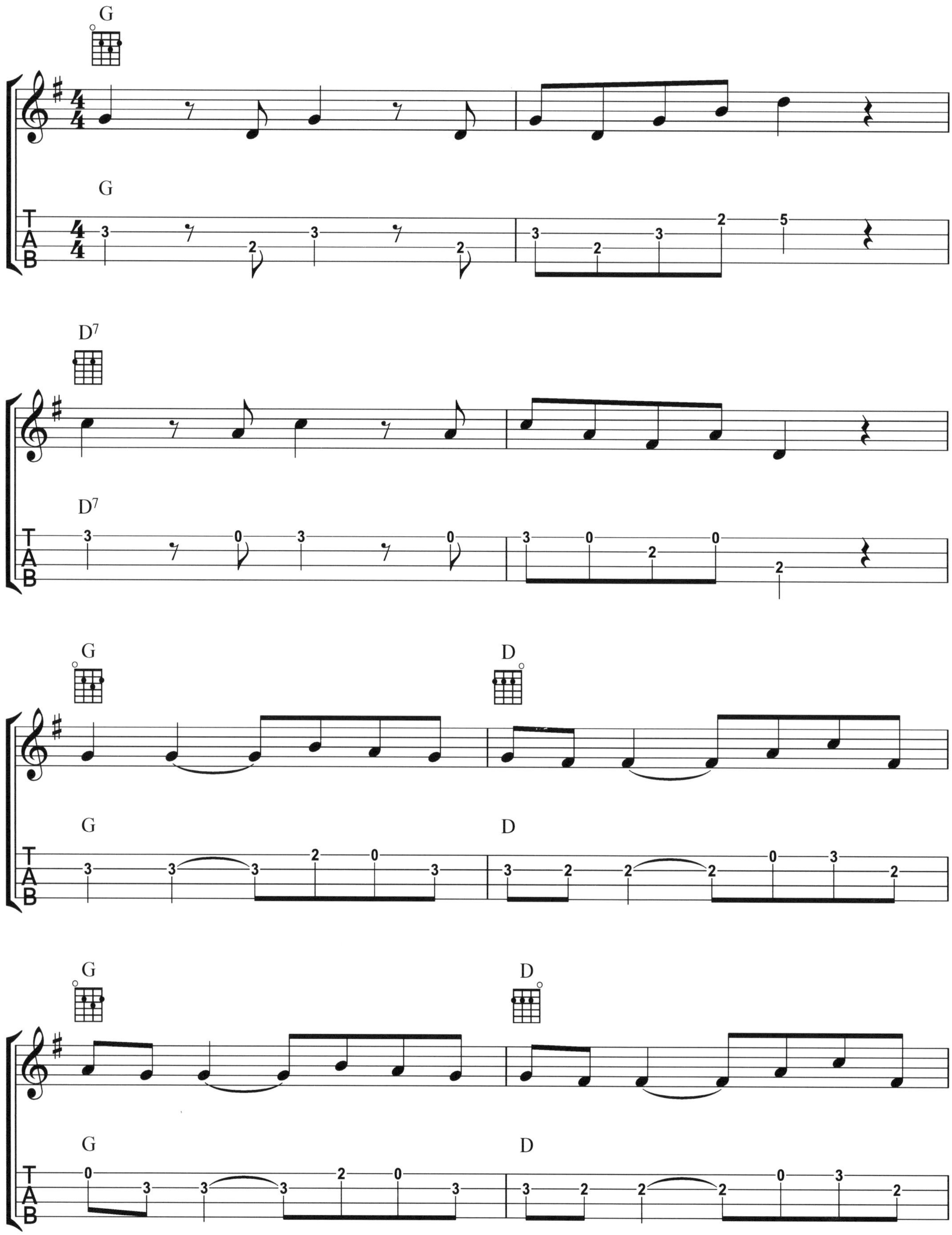

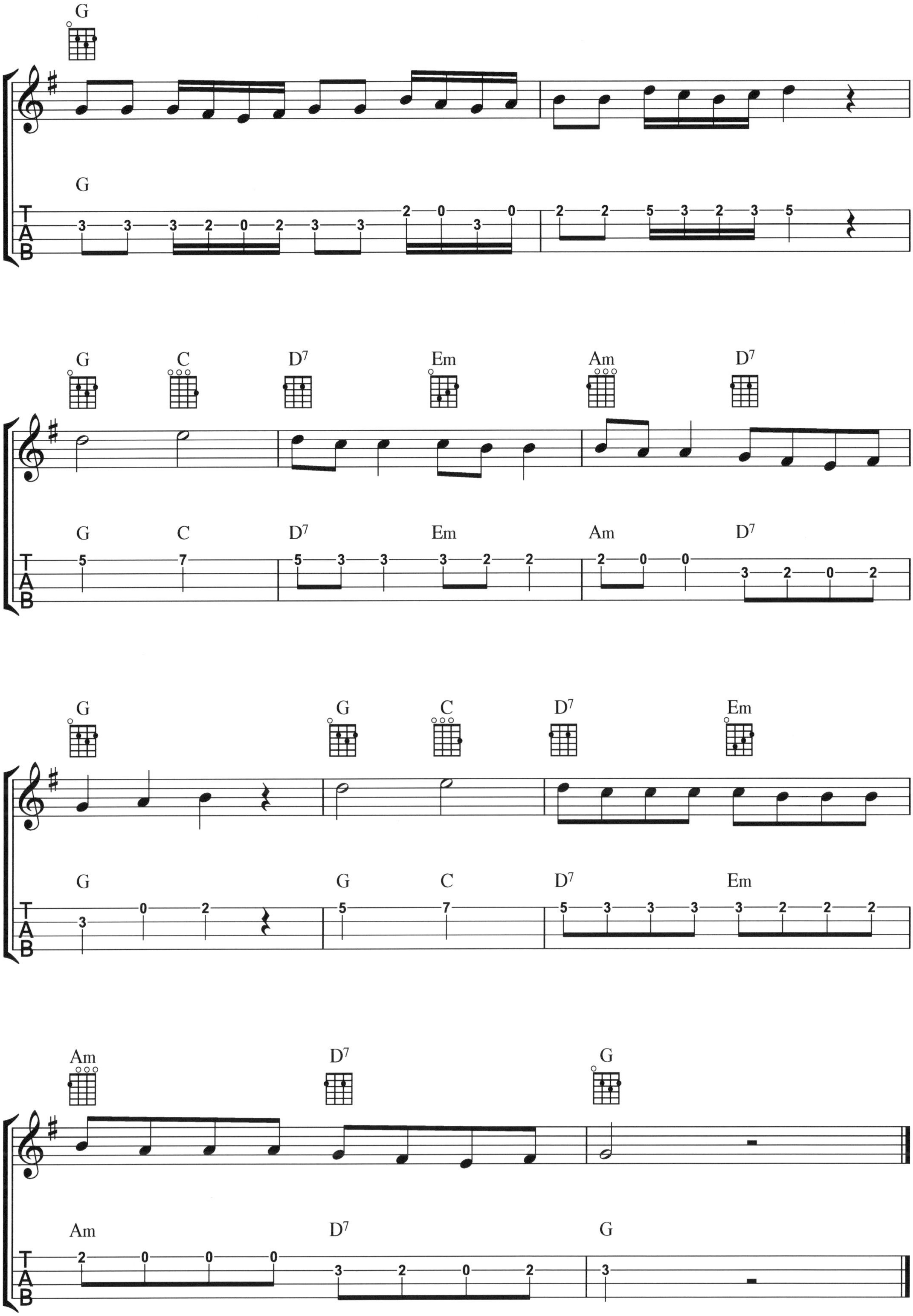
G
G
G C D7 Em Am D7
G C D7 Em Am D7
G G C D7 Em
G G C D7 Em
Am D7 G
Am D7 G

Minuet in A minor

Arranged by David Coe

Henry Purcell

Bridal Chorus

Arranged by David Coe

Richard Wagner

The Merry Farmer

Arranged by David Coe

Robert Schumann

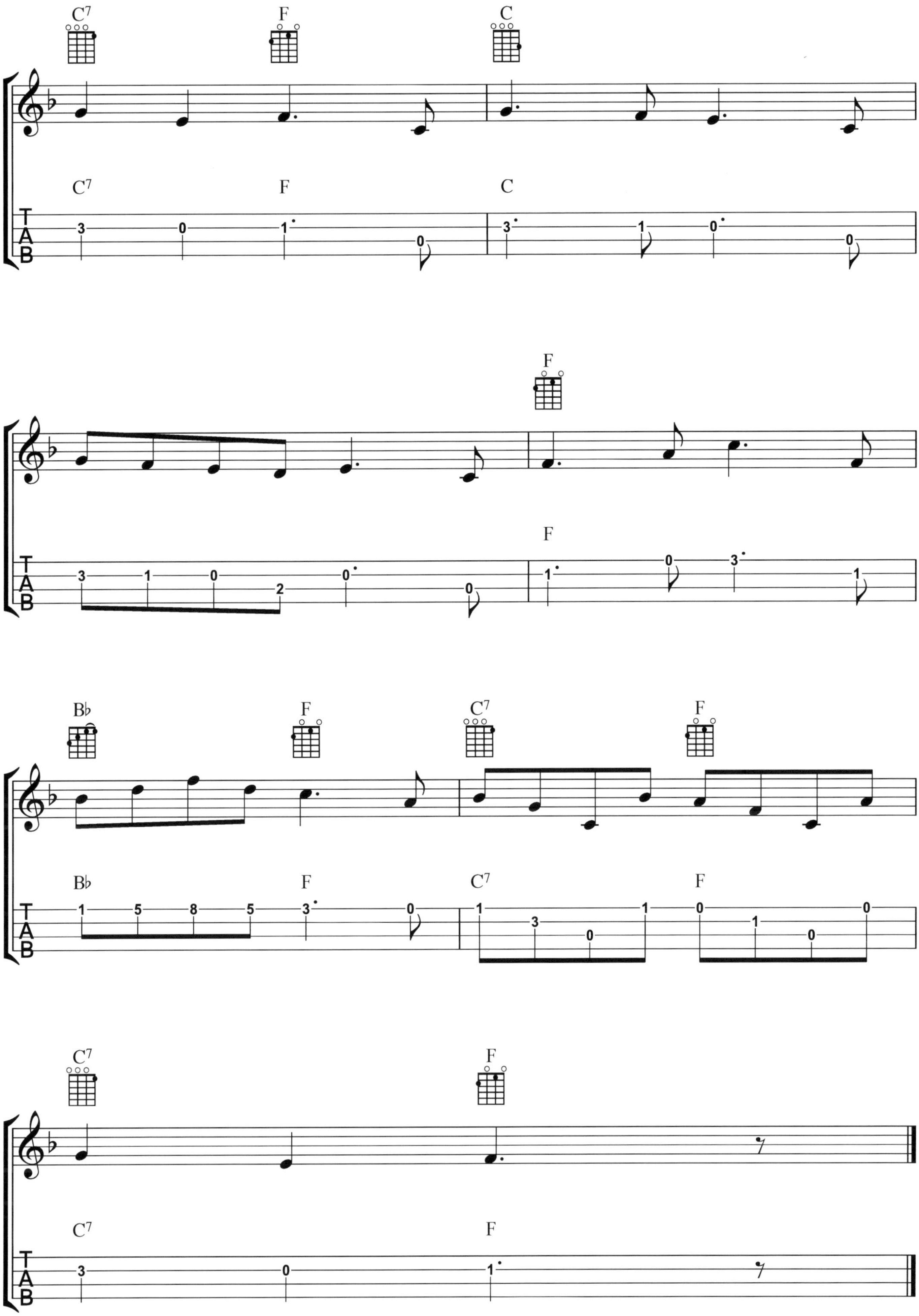
C7 F C
C7 F C
F
F
B♭ F C7 F
B♭ F C7 F
C7 F
C7 F

In a Little French Village

Arranged by David Coe

Peter Ilych Tchaikovsky

Cm Gm Cm F
B♭ Cm B♭ D^7
Gm Cm Gm
Cm Gm D^7 Gm
T
A
B

Greensleeves

Arranged by David Coe

Traditional

C G Em
C G Em
Am F E7
Am F E7
C G Em
C G Em
F E7 Am
F E7 Am

Spring

Arranged by David Coe

Antonio Vivaldi

F B♭ F
F B♭ F
F B♭ F
F B♭ F
B♭ F F C7
B♭ F F C7
F
F

Parade of the Tin Soldiers

Arranged by David Coe

Leon Jessel

G7
C
G7
C
G7
C
Dm
G7
C
Dm
C
G7
C
C
G7
C

Other Recommended Ukulele Books

20 Caribbean Pieces for Ukulele (Carr)
20 Celtic Fingerstyle Uke Tunes (MacKillop)
20 Easy Classical Uke Pieces for Kids (MacKillop)
20 Old-Time American Tunes Arranged for Ukulele (MacKillop)
20 Popular Uke Tunes for Kids (MacKillop)
20 Spanish Baroque Pieces by Gaspar Sanz Arranged for Uke (MacKillop)
Chord Melody Method for Uke (Moore)
Classics for Ukulele (Sarek)
Famous Solos and Duets for the Ukulele (King)
Favorite Fingerstyle Solos for Ukulele (Nelson)
Favorite Old-Time American Songs for Ukulele (Nelson)
Favorite Uke Tunes (N. Jones)
Fingerstyle Duets for Ukulele (Nelson)
Folk Songs for Solo Ukulele (Carr)
Gospel Favorites for Solo Ukulele (Carr)
Great Melodies for Solo Ukulele (Carr)
Hawaiian Uke Tunebook (Eidson/Cherednik)
Holiday Favorites for Solo Ukulele (Carr)
Indie Rock Uke (Driscoll)
Leopold Mozart's Notebook for Wolfgang Arranged for Ukulele (Sarek)
Mauro Giuliani Arranged for Ukulele Duet (Sarek)
Sacred Music for Ukulele (Dempler)
Ten Favorite Hawaiian Songs (Kimura)
The Bach Uke Book (MacKillop)
Uke Tunes Made Easy (W. Bay)
Ukulele Bluegrass Solos (Sarek)
Uke Chords (M. Bay)
Ukulele Duets (Carr)
Ukulele Heaven: Songs from the Golden Age of the Ukulele (Whitcomb)
Ukulele Jamboree! (Whitcomb)
You Can Teach Yourself Ukulele (W. Bay)

WWW.MELBAY.COM